Blessings!
4-25

Jerri Foster Schmidt

THAT FOSTER THING

GUIDING YOUNG WOMEN
THROUGH THE GAME OF LOVE

WESTBOW
PRESS®
A DIVISION OF THOMAS NELSON
& ZONDERVAN

Copyright © 2015 Jerri Foster Schmidt.

All rights reserved. No part of this book may be used or reproduced by any means, graphic, electronic, or mechanical, including photocopying, recording, taping or by any information storage retrieval system without the written permission of the author except in the case of brief quotations embodied in critical articles and reviews.

Scripture taken from the Holy Bible, NEW INTERNATIONAL VERSION®. Copyright © 1973, 1978, 1984, 2011 by Biblica, Inc. All rights reserved worldwide. Used by permission. NEW INTERNATIONAL VERSION® and NIV® are registered trademarks of Biblica, Inc. Use of either trademark for the offering of goods or services requires the prior written consent of Biblica US, Inc.

WestBow Press books may be ordered through booksellers or by contacting:

WestBow Press
A Division of Thomas Nelson & Zondervan
1663 Liberty Drive
Bloomington, IN 47403
www.westbowpress.com
1 (866) 928-1240

Because of the dynamic nature of the Internet, any web addresses or links contained in this book may have changed since publication and may no longer be valid. The views expressed in this work are solely those of the author and do not necessarily reflect the views of the publisher, and the publisher hereby disclaims any responsibility for them.

Any people depicted in stock imagery provided by Thinkstock are models, and such images are being used for illustrative purposes only. Certain stock imagery © Thinkstock.

ISBN: 978-1-5127-1840-9 (sc)
ISBN: 978-1-5127-1841-6 (hc)
ISBN: 978-1-5127-1839-3 (e)

Library of Congress Control Number: 2015918407

Print information available on the last page.

WestBow Press rev. date: 12/07/2015

Contents

Dedication	vii
Preface	ix
Introduction	xiii
1. So This Is Love[1]?	1
2. It Starts Young	7
3. The Purity Covenant	11
4. First Dating Relationship	18
5. You've Got a Friend	25
6. Due Diligence	30
7. Discovering Who You Really Are	37
8. I Think I'm Fallin' for Ya	42
9. That Foster Thing	53
10. To Forgive is Divine	63
11. Misery Loves … Well, Nothing	69
12. Mutual Respect	73
13. The X Factor	90
Endnotes	95

Dedication

This book is lovingly dedicated to my dad, Hal Foster, who is the original Foster in my life, and my mom June Ash Foster who died way too young. Miss you, Mama, every day, since you left us on June 21, 1981.

To my lovely daughter, Kacey: without her none of the book's contents would've taken place. Without her now I would've never figured out my computer enough to write this and hit send.

To my five granddaughters: Mady, Maya, Charly, June, Georgia, and those yet to be born. Jiji loves all her girls.

Last but not least, to my wonderful husband, Tracy Schmidt, who is the love of my life. And who also made it thru the long road of *That Foster Thing* over the last two years and also forty years ago. Wink Wink

Preface

When my daughter Kacey arrived in middle school, I noticed very quickly that things looked a lot different than before. By before, I mean the time when her three older brothers were that age. First of all, it could be said that eleven to twelve-year-old girls are more mature than boys the same age. Whatever. All I know is it's probably the same in every school. The girls seem to go from dolls to makeup with almost no years in between. That's a sad commentary, but let's save that discussion for another book.

The point is girls seem really anxious to grow up and so they just do. I guess I'm saying they rush it. They want to do girl-boy stuff at that age and neither gender is really ready for that world. Many parents go along with it because they think it's inevitable. It may be inevitable, but it doesn't have to be imminent. Again, subject matter for another day; it is what it is.

All I knew was my daughter wasn't ready for all that. Nor was I inclined to accept others' timetables for my child. So I confess

I had a rude awakening. Reinforcing to Kacey how to find like-minded friends quickly followed my deer in the headlights moment.

I had my work cut out for me. The next three to four years were going to be a long road. I had to prepare my child and also handle the teenage culture that we landed in albeit prematurely. When I say we landed in it, it was with a thud. This thud was similar in magnitude to Dorothy's flying house landing in Munchkin Land. Anyway, I knew there must be a way to slow things down in this teenage world that was creeping in on every side. This is where prayer, much prayer, comes in. God says in Ecclesiastes 3:1, "There is a time for everything." I knew He could help us in our journey and, in fact, "He has made everything beautiful in its time" (Ecclesiastes 3:11a). I trusted God that He would do this beautiful thing in Kacey's life.

The next part is what I describe in *That Foster Thing*. I read from Christian experts in the field and then taught her what came naturally for me. I say it was natural because it evolved naturally from what my parents had modeled to me from everyday life. I was hoping to help Kacey steer clear of what appeared to be a ton of pre-teen manufactured drama. This drama left a lot of boys looking like that emoticon with eyes as big as donuts. They truly "didn't know what hit them." Unfortunately, a few years down the road the boys catch up to the girls. I say unfortunately because manipulating pre-teen girls leave a tiny wake compared to the tsunami that mean teen-age boys inflict.

Anyway, I set out to teach Kacey what I believed were timeless principles navigating through romantic relationships. There was not a lot of material out there in Christian bookstores on this exact topic. That's when I knew I wanted to write the book. If only one girl that reads it is spared the pain and heartbreak of lost love, my work has been worth it. If my granddaughters who I dedicate this project to are spared this suffering it's definitely worth it. This is written with love for all of you. Here goes.

Introduction

Have you noticed the epidemic of dysfunctional romantic relationships these days? What's going on? Are people really so unmindful about how to treat those they care about? Maybe they're not in the dark but just selfish. Or maybe they're incapable of truly respecting anyone, even the one they say they love. I've heard of many girls hurt by this kind of behavior from their guys. I wish I could talk to some of those who've been blindsided by this kind of "love."

Would you say you are one of those girls? If so, there's hope for your next dating experience. It never feels good to be done wrong by someone you anticipated would be different than the others. If it were possible to be clued in on your boyfriend's motives, would you want that? I would. That's why *That Foster Thing* can help. There's information in the pages that follow that can give early insight as to the lifespan of the new relationship. Armed with this information, you won't be surprised when things play out one way or the other.

I hope *That Foster Thing* will show girls and young women that there's hope for them when they face romantic conflict. A good dose of old-fashioned confidence and self-respect can go a long way. Hopefully this book will help put girls "in the know" about what could be described as the roller coaster of love. It has its ups, its downs, and its whiplash surprises. At the end of it all, you can be anywhere from thrilled and breathless to dizzy and nauseous.

I'd love for you to be thrilled, but not so much the other adjectives. If you were elated, as being thrilled suggests, it would mean things are probably working out in your love life. The tips contained in this read are meant to help in the coaching department. That means that you evaluate the actions and reactions of your new guy and respond accordingly. It's having a starring role in the whole experience and not playing victim ever again.

I don't propose manipulating or trying to control anyone. Ever. The only person I advocate controlling is yourself. And this kind of control actually gives freedom and inspires confidence. People who know you may be so surprised at your new attitude they may not recognize you. Your dating history is just that. History. There's a new girl in town!

The sad truth is many girls have romantic relationships that seem to mirror each other. That means they tend to last about the same length of time because the excitement fades way too soon, and they end the same way as the others. Unsatisfying would be the appropriate word here. Expected would be another. This is because it's human nature to do the same things over and over. Well no more. *That Foster Thing* is *especially* for those girls. If this describes you, then read on, herein lies help.

1

So This Is Love?

I have observed so many girls and women, young and old, who seem to be involved in romantic relationships that are mediocre, at best. I wanted something much better than that for my children and, now, for my grandchildren as well. My intention is to share my observations of romance among females of all ages but mostly the young and inexperienced.

No matter who you are or what your background may be, opening up to romance can leave you exhilarated, overwhelmed, confused, discouraged, or any combination thereof. I strive to share how to live as a Christ-honoring teen or young person through the dating experience. I also address navigating through some of the unavoidable things boy–girl relationships bring. These things would better be described as "bumps in the road." Said bumps come unexpectedly, because they are the result of young people's new thoughts and experiences. They may be predictable and completely expected among the older set, because they've already been around the love merry-go-round. By default, those new to the interworking of romance are also new to its pitfalls. That's why this book is written mainly to them.

There's a strong case to be made that teens need guidance about these issues simply because they are new to them. The feelings that go with dating can be staggering and confusing. While these feelings could be described as organic and spontaneous, they are not completely unpredictable. Truths and principles can be applied to add some clarity and maybe even a little confidence.

Nothing would sadden me more than to hear my granddaughters went the same path I see so many heartsick people trudge. On the other hand, what great joy would be mine to hear my grandchildren went the route of their parents, who all married very well. I'm so grateful to God for all my children and their spouses. They've all made commitments to our Lord and Savior Jesus Christ and are living out their faith in Him. Now they are raising their own children in that faith. All praise be to the Lord!

Now, back to the common occurrence that seems to describe so many unfulfilling dating relationships. When it comes to love, why are so many Christians having the same dissatisfying experiences as their lost neighbors? Do we really not know any better? As Christians, we should know better. Instead, our Christianity doesn't seem to be enough reason for us to treat those we love with grace. It should be, mind you, but it's not. Why?

One reason we act the same as those without Christ is that we don't obey the Word of the God we say we serve. If we did, there wouldn't be all this pain and estrangement between people who supposedly love each other. Maybe we don't even know the Word of our God. "Be kind and compassionate to one another, forgiving each other, just as in Christ God forgave you" (Ephesians 4:32 NIV) should be our mantra. Instead, it's read, maybe memorized in Sunday school as a child, and then forgotten when needed most.

Another reason is we don't have a healthy view of ourselves. If we did, we'd establish boundaries from the outset. Those boundaries would give us freedom and set parameters. They would, by definition, have stopping points in a number of areas inside the new romance. Your first thought may be physical stopping points. While that is certainly part of it, and we'll discuss it more later, there are many others.

First, how you actually treat each other should have boundaries. Many girls have tolerated bad treatment at the hands of their boyfriends for so long they don't even realize it's happening. They've grown to accept it and maybe even think they deserve no better. It could be they didn't grow up seeing their father treat their mother with kindness. Without seeing it modeled before them, it might seem completely foreign to expect it.

We need to show others that we value ourselves and are worthy of respect. In matters of love, we need go no further than the Bible to see God's view. I John 4:7–8 says, "Dear friends, let us love one another, for love comes from God. Everyone who loves has been born of God and knows God. Whoever does not love does not know God, because God is love."

Many people use the word *love* to describe how they feel for their boyfriends or girlfriends. I argue that

Love sweet love.

calling it love might be like calling a sand castle a beach or calling a rock a mountain. Not to completely discount their strong feelings of affection, I propose we try to see love in more of a spiritual light, as referred to in 1 John 4:7. Can we really know love without God? Can teenagers feel the depths of something God calls *love*? After all, He is the Creator of love.

If what this world needs now is love, sweet love[2] (lyrics from an old Jackie DeShannon song), at least the Christians should start looking and living like it. After all, if there's no hope or example in Christians for the world to see, there's no hope for anyone.

I believe there is hope for Christians. There is hope in more areas than just love. Jesus is our hope in love and life. Without Him, we have no real life, much less love. So rejoice, sisters, we have Jesus Christ, who comes to us and never leaves or forsakes us. He desires that we show the world what love looks like.

I write this to mothers and daughters alike. You'll notice I go back and forth between the young and the not-so-young. That's intentional on my part. I write to mothers, because they realize how critical it is to marry the right man. They know this, because they either did or didn't do so themselves. If these mothers are like me, they want all the help they can find to steer their daughters correctly. I would truly love it if young people/daughters would read this. I mentioned already that I want to shed some light on this subject, even if that light is a small illumination. If no one is offering young girls guidance,

Jerri Foster Schmidt

they need this info to make prayerful decisions. I hope by the time you finish this book, you'll say, "Anything I can do to help my daughter find her true love, with God's help and leading, I will do." Or if you're a young girl, I pray you'll realize your worth in God's economy. He says you're worth dying for.

2

It Starts Young

I believe most people start forming habits of how they will treat possible boyfriends or girlfriends when they first experience puppy love. That playful, exciting time usually occurs in middle school. That's between eleven and thirteen years of age. That's young, but it's traditionally the age kids wake up to this strange, new world of the opposite sex.

If your daughter is younger than eleven and already into boys, that's not a good thing. When I say "into" boys, I'm not implying it's okay after eleven if she's preoccupied with boys. I'm just saying it's normal to be interested in the opposite sex at that age. When my daughter, Kacey, was that age, she became interested, not surprisingly. She was super comfortable around boys because she has three older brothers. Even though boys did not intimidate her, I still didn't want her to be unwittingly thrust into an attraction dynamic she wasn't ready for.

All girls need instruction from someone who cares about them, preferably their mother (but it doesn't have to be) about these creatures called boys. Many grown women never had anyone mentor them about romantic relationships, nor did they seem to learn on their own. As a result, they suffered preventable heartache. How to lose a guy in thirty days became their unhappy experience time and again. For some unwitting females, this has become their byline. Said another way, "unlucky in love," or "a train wreck when it comes to romance," becomes synonymous with their names.

Just like some movies we've all seen, they do the very thing men hate. Then the poor guy just wants to run away from the girl—or woman. Such a girl starts chasing the guy, which pushes him even further away. He now sees her in a completely different light. She's lost a lot of self-respect in the process. She possibly doesn't even know she's disrespected herself. If she knew, maybe she wouldn't have ended up like this. I venture to say she has no idea what happened. It doesn't matter, though, because now he's long gone, and she's heartbroken. This book is for that girl—the one with no idea why she continues to lose her guy.

I believe some girls invite heartbreak and misery by the way they act toward their boyfriends. I think a girl can actually push a boyfriend away, unintentionally of course, by chasing him and being too clingy. This tends to turn him away from

That Foster Thing

her. Many times he doesn't even realize why she doesn't excite him anymore. Frequently, she starts telling him what to do. The relationship becomes defined by her desires and explicit instructions and, thus, declines. It is the most common thing for girls to do, because they think they can, and their friends tell them they should. They say, "Just tell him what you want him to do. He needs you to tell him!" It may also be the "little mother" in her, rearing its premature, misguided head. What a shame! This is her first step in disrespecting him by treating him not like an equal but like a child.

Going back, and using my own family as an example, I'll start before my daughter dated. When Kacey was about eleven years old, I noticed that a lot of girls her age were into planning their lives and the lives of their friends. Let me say a word here about the kind of girls that I wanted as friends for my daughter.

First of all, I wanted her to have Christian friends because we are believers and followers of Christ. Next, I steered her away from those who lied to her or to their own parents. I told Kacey, "If a girl lies to you or you hear her lie to her parents, she does not need to be one of your closest friends. If she tells you of lying to her parents, teachers, or friends, again, not best friend material."

I also did not want my daughter to be swept into this world of constant planning done by middle-schoolers. Parties and get-togethers are great for preteens, but they need to be special and not every weekend. It seems to me that a lot of these young girls start dreaming up activities that include boys and want their parents to just consent because everyone is doing it. Well, not me. I wanted to slowly let my child start experiencing some freedoms, but not at the whims of some twelve–year-old party planner.

Many parents of preteeners are tired, it appears, and don't want to finish the job of raising their children. So, ipso facto, the kids start deciding for themselves what their schedule will look like.

Also, I didn't want Kacey with what I saw as the future *fast crowd*. I've noticed that kids that get into the adult world too young, too soon get burned out with age-appropriate movies, parties, TV, and so on. Not that there's a lot to choose from in appropriate media as is. Plus, I wanted her to be around boys that were being raised like her brothers. That meant we needed to take these next few years and observe, pray, and go little by little.

3

The Purity Covenant

When our kids turned thirteen, my husband and I did a covenant talk with them about their value in Christ and their value to us. We had already explained about the beauty of God-created sex but also the dangers of illicit, unmarried sex. Yes, we're old-fashioned. We wanted our kids to wait for marriage to have sex. I'm not apologizing for our stance on this. We were, and are, very comfortable with our convictions on this issue.

We used a special covenant dinner to lead them to a prayer of commitment to God for their purity. The night ended with us presenting them with a gift of remembrance to seal their heart-felt decisions. With Kacey, it was a diamond heart necklace that she could wear on future dates that would remind her of the commitment she had made to God. As I implied before, our boys made covenant decisions also.

Do kids who make a purity commitment wait for marriage before having sex? Some probably don't, but they have a better chance of it after being lovingly taught and encouraged to do so. They have also committed it to God, so they have the Holy Spirit to help them in weak times. I Corinthians 10:13 says, "No temptation has seized you except what is common to man. And God is faithful; He will not let you be tempted beyond what you can bear. But when you are tempted, He will also provide a way out so that you can stand up under it." There you have it! God's word confirms His faithfulness when we are tempted.

Remember the Bible story of Joseph with Potiphar's wife? If you need a refresher, it's in Genesis 39. After Joseph refuses to have sex with Mrs. Potiphar, he runs out of the house to get away from her. According to verse 12, even the honorable, God-fearing Joseph had to flee temptation. On our best day, we are not stronger in the flesh than the noble Joseph. God gives us this example to see that running away from sinful sexual invitation is a good idea.

I want to say a word about the concept of running away. When someone runs, that person is trying to get away fast. There's no time to talk about whether it's a good idea. There's no time to talk about why it's a bad idea. Joseph felt the urgency to flee, and he was spot on. He knew that too much time in Mrs. Potiphar's grip spelled disaster, and he acted quickly. Joseph's reaction showed what a wise man he was. One reason for his wisdom was that God was his companion. We see several times in the Bible where it says the Lord was with Joseph. In particular it says this in verses 2, 21, and 23 of chapter 39. We should never think that our God is not a God of the details. His example from Scripture in Joseph's life is vividly clear.

Does this mean Christians always overcome temptation? No, not even close. Does this mean by the power of the Holy Spirit they can? Absolutely! Does any of this mean we know for sure if our kids stay pure? No, we don't know. We can ask them if they are staying true to their covenant, which, by the way, I recommend. We should also pray for them earnestly.

I know you may be thinking they would probably just lie to their parents. After all, doesn't everyone lie about unmarried sex? Most in the Christian community would lie, I think. Again, there's no way to be completely sure, but asking them is a way to help them be accountable. Being accountable, as a teen, is a good thing. It could be an added motivator to be pure. After all, what true Christian, teen, or otherwise wants to repeatedly lie to someone who cares about him or her and is trying to help?

What does being pure mean anyway? Some Christians have, rather crudely, said it means "hands on hands and lips on lips." This is not a handbook on the allowed and unallowed in the area of intimacy for unmarried Christians. It does, however, demand addressing for those who are new Christians or have no clue how to navigate this issue with all the sexual pollution that exists in our current-day media. Both parties need to be committed to sexual purity. To expand on that, don't do anything that you couldn't do in front of your parents, stay out of situations that could make you fall or compromise on your commitment, and pray for the Holy Spirit to help you avoid pitfalls. If you avoid the appearance of impropriety, you are, in fact, avoiding impropriety (anything improper).

Don't underestimate your need to pray about this. Believe me, everything in the world today, including but not limited to TV, movies, the internet, pop culture, literature, music, society, celebrities, friends, and even some adults will be working against you. It will truly be a "God thing" if you're able to stay sexually pure before marriage.

I don't want to leave this topic without saying a couple more things. First, be careful what you put in your mind. Philippians 4:8 says, "Whatever is true, whatever is noble, whatever is right, whatever is pure, whatever is lovely, whatever is admirable-if anything is excellent or praiseworthy-think about such things." In other words, fill your mind with pure things or things that can be praised.

That Foster Thing

I remember when Kacey started dating her now-husband, Brandon. My husband and I knew him to be an honorable young man and felt good about their dating. Kacey had told me, after an evening out with Brandon, how special she had felt when, during half time at a pro basketball game when the cheerleaders danced onto the court for their performance, Brandon turned and looked at her. He talked to Kacey the whole time and never turned his head to even look at the scantily clad girls at the center of everyone's attention. We all knew then that Brandon was the kind of young man who would be a blessing not only to our daughter but also to our whole family as well.

There's one last thing I want to cover on this issue. Let's say you've found some value in what's been talked about so far. Let's say further that you have gotten some ideas for direction in your own life or for a girl you are mentoring. Some reading this might say, "It's too late. I've (or my daughter has) already gone too far sexually." Make no mistake; it is never too late for anyone to make a new commitment to themselves and God and to be pure going forward. Our God is in the business of forgiving. It's one of the most unhuman (divine) things He does. Nehemiah 9:17b says, "You are a forgiving God, gracious and compassionate, slow to anger and abounding in love." First John 1:9 says, "If we confess our sins, He is faithful and just and will forgive us our sins and purify us from all unrighteousness." The Bible is filled with declarations of His love, compassion, and forgiveness of His children. I love the way God takes us as we are and helps us when we don't know how to help ourselves. Thank you, dear Lord, for not treating us as our sins deserve.

The Bible is the only book that reads you.

Psalm 103:10–17 says, "He does not treat us as our sins deserve or repay us according to our iniquities. For as high as the heavens are above the earth, so great is His love for those who fear Him; as far as the east is from the west, so far has He removed our transgressions from us. As a father has compassion on his children, so the Lord has compassion on those who fear Him; for He knows how we are formed, He remembers that we are dust. As for man, his days are like grass, he flourishes like a flower of the field; the wind blows over it and it is gone, and its place remembers it no more. But from everlasting to everlasting the Lord's love is with those who fear Him, and His righteousness with their children's children."

There is nothing you can do that God cannot forgive. No one human is perfect, certainly not me, my family, or any other person whose life experiences are discussed in this book. I know of no one whose dating life, or life before or since, has been without error. As they say, the ground is level at the foot of the cross, which means all people are sinners, and all sinners need forgiveness. If anyone asks Jesus to forgive his or her sins, He will do it. He desires oneness with His children, and you can call on Him no matter where you are. Don't delay. He's a whisper away.

4

First Dating Relationship

Now, some people may think fifteen is old enough to start "car dating." I think it's still too young for reasons I will get into more in this chapter. Remember that attraction dynamic I referred to? Well, it can be very powerful, and it's not for the faint of heart. What I mean is the first attraction experience for the opposite sex can be unexpected and completely unsettling to the point of total distraction. It can throw older people completely off kilter. Imagine what it does to teenagers! It has the potential to completely rock their world! As parents, you want as much maturity as possible in your children when they make their dating debut. That means you don't see any signs of them becoming obsessive or "being in love" when they have their first date.

The love may very well come for your daughter with this young person, but she should not go into it with that mindset. And if it *is* love, it will grow over a period of years of taking one step at a time and God drawing their hearts together. Trust me, you want that to be God's handiwork and not their own engineering. More than likely, this will just end up being someone you will remember as the first one your daughter went on a date with, not your son-in-law.

It would never be a mistake to *not* start dating at fifteen for the reasons just outlined. However, a strong case can be made for it being a mistake to start dating at that age. You know your child. You, not she, should be the one to decide she is ready. To be cautious, I would rather err on the side of being safe. For our daughter, my husband and I decided that around sixteen was the age we were shooting for. That means by today's standards, they are mature and very responsible. Some may say it is impossible to make your daughter wait that long. I disagree. Yes, it's rare in today's time, but it can be done. I truly felt my daughter was ready. Even more important than her maturity is the fact that you trust her. You've had all the talks about the birds and the bees, about purity, and about being chaste. Again, you trust her. I cannot overstate this. Trust is something you either have in her or you don't.

Birds don't wait till they're 16 to date.

Just be careful to know when to tell your daughter, "You're not ready yet, darling. You will be soon!" And if you say that, mean it. Mean it by adhering to what you feel like God has shown you about your child's maturity. It's much easier to hold your daughter back than to let her start dating and then have to pull her back because you see she's not handling it very well. Set her up for success. You'll be so glad you did.

A Christian friend once said about the people her daughter was hanging out with, "I don't like them, but I don't know why. I don't know anything specific. I just know I don't like them. They're all older, and they won't really look me in the eye." These people were eighteen, and her daughter was fifteen. That's a big age gap in the teenage world. Her daughter had already been in trouble, and I knew why this mother was worried. I had noticed her daughter was picking up some behaviors that were destructive.

I said to her, "It doesn't matter if you don't know anything specific. She's your daughter, and you don't feel good about who she wants to leave the house with. I would not let her go." I hope you're seeing what I was seeing. It really should never come to the point of a Christian mother worrying because her child has decided to go out with someone untrustworthy. When that happens, you need to back up. Way back. At that point, your child is not following the path you've prayed she would follow.

First of all, hopefully, you've taught your child to recognize desirable and undesirable traits in her friends. Second, you should have already okayed whom she was going out with anyway. Next, the most important issue in parenting is that the Holy Spirit is our unseen Helper when we can't see into the heart and mind of someone. He wants to protect our child just as much, if not more, than we do. When you are praying and trusting in the Lord's help with your daughter's dating life, why would He ever be in the business of putting your child with someone you don't have peace about? I'll tell you plainly, He wouldn't! So, if you don't feel good about it, then as we used to say when our kids were teenagers, "It ain't happening!" Your daughter is too precious to put in the wrong hands.

Lastly, she needs to learn to trust you. Yes, I just turned that trust issue around. She needs to trust and value the judgment of her parents. Nobody on earth cares more about her, her welfare, and her happiness than her mother and father. They would never lead her astray, right? Right! So why parents go awol when it comes to this I will never know. *Awol* is a military term that means absent without leave. Leave is considered your permission from your officer to leave the base. If a parent is awol, he or she has abdicated or neglected his or her responsibility to the child and to God. Let's just call it what it is: it's being an absentee parent. After all, God gave this child to you, and He trusts you with her. So mothers, stop being silent about your child's friends! This issue is too important to ignore.

I don't want to move on without saying a word about your daughter's confidence in her parents' judgment. There's a good chance that you and your child will not always agree about who's dateable. In fact, you can count on it! This is where her respect for your opinion is both coveted and necessary. As the mom of a minor, you get to call the shots on your child's activities, but I hope she seeks your blessing about the matter anyway. God will always bless her for honoring her parents in this way.

That Foster Thing

Don't let your heart carry you away.

If you say no to your daughter's desire to date someone, you may have a lapse in your peaceful household. That's okay. Better to get it right on this. God can change your heart if you've gotten it wrong, and you haven't trusted her judgment where you should have. She should submit to the decision of your God-given authority and pray for God to change your hearts.

Mothers, you should value your daughter's opinion by this time too. If you have every reason to trust her, then pray for God to open your heart to His leading if you've been mistaken. When in doubt, take the time to be sure. No crime there. If this potential date is worthy, he will want your approval. For that reason, he will be willing to wait if he really wants to date your daughter. It would be especially nice if he asked you for permission to date her. It's not mandatory though. Hopefully, you will already know the boy who's getting close enough to be interested in your daughter that way. For that reason, as the parent, you should see this coming and not be blindsided by it.

5

You've Got a Friend

By now you've explained the beauty and sacredness of marital sex and warned about the dangers of casual sex. You've also tried to hold onto the reins of your daughter's blossoming social life. Now, how do you help her find the right ones to date?

Assuming you are praying for the Holy Spirit's help to bring a nice Christian boy into the picture, do not settle for anything less. Church rows are filled with those poor girls and women who have settled. They've settled for guys who said they were Christians, yet they were very much entrenched in the world's ideas about free sex. These guys may be believers in Christ; that's not for me to judge. Being a "Christian" in the world's eyes may not be enough in this case.

Our kids' youth leader once said, "When it comes to who your child dates, being a Christian is not enough. That person needs to be a 'growing Christian.'" Now, we could talk for a couple of chapters about why every Christian should be a growing Christian. We could even dispute the Christianity altogether of someone who is not growing in faith. We could also find many examples of people who said they were true followers of Christ, yet their faith did not seem to direct them to a godly lifestyle. That is not for me to judge. I must decide, however, while I can affect my child's choices, to help her look for someone who's set apart from the rest.

Next, pray that you'll be aware of any red flags. Red flags, to me, are those little negative things that let you in on the character of a person. Lying is a red flag. Picking dishonorable people as best friends is another one. My mom used to say, "Birds of a feather flock together." That, of course, was not original with her, but she used it a lot to speak to how people hang around with those they either like or aspire to be like. A person's choice of buddies, most times, tells you something about them.

The Bible plainly says in I Corinthians 15:33, "Bad company corrupts good character." This verse is extremely clear, and the Bible does not lie. If you try to override (set aside) this truth, beware! You're never as strong as you think, and I have found that spiritual truths are not something a person can void or avoid. God says He will not be mocked. Galatians 6:7–8 says, "Do not be deceived: God cannot be mocked. A man reaps what he sows. The one who sows to please his sinful nature, from that nature will reap destruction; the one who sows to please the Spirit, from the Spirit will reap eternal life." And verse 9 is a great conclusion. Galatians 6:9 says, "Let us not become weary in doing good, for at the proper time we will reap a harvest if we do not give up."

What better motivation could we have? God is saying to keep on doing the right thing. You will be blessed! Do not give up!

I did not forbid my kids to be friends with those not like them, but again, I did not want them as my children's closest friends. However, if there were numerous red flags with those friends, I tried to curtail my children's involvement with them completely. Over the years I've seen many good kids brought down by the bad kids. It's a sad thing to watch. A very sad thing.

I once heard our church children's director caution new parents that if you let your child hang around the bad kids on the block in hopes of converting them to Christianity, usually you end up with your kids picking up the bad behavior and the neighbors still being lost. The point here is not that we shouldn't witness and involve ourselves in the lives of those who need Christ. But we adults know how to do that without putting our kids out there to do it for us. They're learning, after all, how to live out their faith. They're kids. And guess what? Teenagers need our help with this too. Also, the other part of that statement is a truth that we've surely learned when our children were mere toddlers. That is, kids pick up behaviors of those around them so fast it will make your head spin! There's a reason why mimicking is referred to as "aping." Not a great picture, for sure.

So, in summation, in a loving way, teach your child how to look for indicators of what convictions, if any, her friends are living by. This is not to condemn them but is a mental note of who might be potentially better friends for them.

Meet the Parents

Another area to explore lies in the arena of parents. We could talk all day and list many godly parents who raised what appear to be infidels. So sad. After all, we have no greater joy than to hear that our children walk in the truth (see 3 John 4). Conversely, as a Christian parent, we have no greater sorrow than to know our child has rejected Christ.

It's easy to see why so many people turn out the way they do when you look at who raised them. In many cases, "the apple doesn't fall far from the tree." I've also seen numerous Christian parents just dabble in some immoral behavior, thinking it's not a big deal. Of course, it *is* a big deal because our kids watch us to see if we are genuine. They want to see us living the life we're teaching them to live. Any inconsistencies in our lives are surely noticed by those living in the same house. No surprise there. It's been said that what we parents do in moderation, our kids will do in excess. How true! I've seen this over and over. We're not perfect parents, but we have a job to be real before our children, and we need to be faithful.

Of course, there's always those loving Christian parents who have labored to raise their children in a God-honoring home, but the children did not accept their God. Again, sad. Also, there are great stories of how God redeemed the life of someone raised in brokenness and dysfunction. That person went on to a great life lived for God despite their childhood. With our God, the impossible becomes possible, (see Matthew 19:26). So, the parents are an indicator, a big one usually, about the home and their children.

6

Due Diligence

Before feeling good about or giving your approval for your daughter to date someone, take into consideration the following: where the boy goes to church, what outside activities he's involved in, who his friends are, who his parents are, what his character is like, and of course, the Holy Spirit's leading.

The issue about where he goes to church is important because what he believes about God is critical. Sometimes, even among Christians, things a person subscribes to regarding religion might be a showstopper or "date stopper," as it were. It helps if you can know the big differences in this area before you consent for your daughter to date someone. If he goes to church somewhere you're familiar with, it's either something that's okay with you or not. Christians can have differing views about what is acceptable, and usually those views are preached in one's church.

That Foster Thing

For example, is what a Christian believes about alcohol consumption a hill to die on? I'm not referring to underage drinking of alcohol here. It would be natural to assume that most Christians would be law-abiding citizens, and therefore, be against illegal drinking by minors. On the other hand, I wasn't born yesterday. I know that teenagers drink. I also know that many Christian teenagers drink.

There are obviously many reasons to not want your daughter dating a drinker. If under the influence, everything from his diminished ability to drive a car to his possible increased desire for sex comes to mind as problems. Either of these side effects, including a whole host of others—all negative—could ensue. We don't need to discuss teenagers' drinking and driving. Enough on that.

For the purposes of the compatibility discussion, let's touch on drinking alcohol in general. This would refer to the use of it for adults. Let's say you believe a Christian should be set apart from the world to the point of never partaking in strong drink. You might even believe that the drinking of alcohol in scripture was a much-diluted version compared to today's drink. For that reason, your family abstains from using alcohol. Conversely, your daughter's friend believes drinking is not important one way or the other. Let's say his family does drink and goes to a church where using alcohol is not frowned upon or even discussed. There are, after all, many differing views on the subject among God-fearing people. These would be described as people who want to live a life of righteousness and have a strong witness to the presence of Christ in their life. We are not their judges. We have enough to worry about tending to our own downfalls without trying to pick specks from the eyes of others.

Having said all that, you feel the way you feel. Do you see this as a big problem in the future? Does this make you want to prevent the relationship from moving forward? In some cases, families have been hurt as a result of alcohol abuse, and for that reason, they steer clear of alcohol altogether. This is a question best asked when their relationship starts growing closer than just "friends."

If there are no roadblocks with the points from the first paragraph of this chapter, you can, with fear and trembling, consent to let him be around your daughter. I know I seem hesitant about it, even now. A vivid picture comes to mind of an illustration our former pastor, Adrian Rogers, used. He said, "Letting your daughter date is like taking a Stradivarius violin and putting it in the hands of a gorilla." Nice image, huh? That *is* the way we feel. Our daughters are our most prized possession, along with our sons. We have put too much into training them and coaching them to handle this very important thing too casually. So, we consent to that boy who stands out.

It's easy to stand with a boy who stands out.

Now, can you cover every base? Let me be the first to say you can't. Why? We've gone to all these pains, and still this might not be foolproof? Unfortunately it is not. That's because teenagers are just the younger set of a fickle breed called people. People mess up. Even Christians mess up. We are masters at being double-minded.

Now that doesn't mean this is a character trait; it just means we have moments in our lives that are hypocritical to who we say we are or what we believe. I think it's just the humanness of us all.

Even the Apostle Paul struggled with this. He said in Romans 7:15, "I do not understand what I do. For what I want to do I do not do, but what I hate I do."

When I notice this in my own life, I tell my husband, "I feel like a Paulina (female Paul) today. What I want to do, I do not do."

Having established that our frailties are as common to man today as thousands of years ago, suffice it to say, we're not perfect. So expecting perfection from someone who dates our daughter is futile. Having said that, we do expect him to be exceptional. We also expect him to be honorable and to treat our daughter with respect. By the way, we expect her to do the same. We'll get more into this later.

The Wish List

To sum up, what traits are we looking for in a boyfriend?

1. He's a growing Christian. He's actively involved in a personal relationship with Christ—the most important thing on the list.
2. He's committed to preserving his and his girlfriend's sexual purity.
3. He's honorable and is trustworthy always to tell the truth.
4. He's diligent in academics or vocation, or both, and strives to find God's direction for his future.

That Foster Thing

As a former scoutmaster's daughter, I would love to say the requirements for a good Boy Scout are expected. Until now they've been unspoken. I'll list them now as a starting point.

The Boy Scout Law says a scout is trustworthy, loyal, helpful, friendly, courteous, kind, obedient, cheerful, thrifty, brave, clean, and reverent.

If a young man possesses these attributes in addition to the cream-of-the-crop things previously listed, he's probably a dream—figuratively and realistically.

We know he'll have faults, and he won't be perfect, just as we mothers and daughters are not perfect. We can, however, strive for excellence in ourselves and desire it in our future mates.

You Aren't Going to Wear That, Are You?

All this time you're preparing your daughter for her future in the dating world. Coaching her in the area of dress is one place to concentrate on. This is a good time to make her aware of how her clothes tell others about her.

Good or bad, our outward adornment says a lot. It can say, "I'm going to show a little cleavage here to get the attention of this cute guy." More preferably, it will say, "I need to make sure this top is not too tight or too revealing. I don't want to give the wrong impression."

I think many girls and women have no idea how they are viewed by the opposite sex. Men are such visual creatures and can be lured by Satan to impure thinking when they see too much female skin.

Some girls know this and use it to lure boys. Some girls know this and don't care because they're not concerned with anyone's purity. Some girls don't know this and unwittingly lure boys, and those boys don't know the girl didn't know what she did. Some girls know this, they care about it, and they dress accordingly. By this I mean they try not to lead someone on.

You might need to be creative sometime, but you don't have to dress matronly to be discreet. You can dress cute and still cover what you need to cover. Many conservative women have had to put many a cute item back on the rack because it showed too much, and they didn't want to be seen that way. I mean that two ways. They didn't want to show that much skin, and they didn't want others to perceive them as provocative. It's much better to teach girls to have the attention drawn to their face, or better yet, a winsome spirit, not to their body.

7

Discovering Who You Really Are

We've covered a lot about finding those guys who are dateable for our girls. We've also talked about our girls being the right kind of date for those guys. Now to the ins and outs of early dating.

I've seen many girls who don't appear to realize how their actions are running guys off. I call it the "neediness syndrome." It manifests itself by these girls putting their whole lives into this new relationship. This is not marriage. It's dating. Big difference.

Most girls attract a guy in the beginning by, hopefully, being themselves. Some boy-obsessed girls try to be someone else in hopes of luring a particular guy. I'm not even talking about those girls. They are on a confused, midnight train to nowhere.

I'm focused on that girl who is genuinely wanting to find God's person for her. This particular boy has been uniquely gifted by God to complement her strengths and weaknesses. If this is a relationship born in heaven, it will be something good for everyone involved. You might say, "I'm not looking for my daughter to find 'the one' right now. We're just talking about her dating around."

Dating around can be dangerous because it may let too many guys in too close. We don't want differing dating views influencing our young, impressionable daughters. The dating standards I'm proposing will be radically conservative compared to your daughter's peers, and for that reason, you have to control the negatives as much as possible. Oh, if we could only know where and who the big negatives were. Sometimes it will be obvious, sometimes not. It's those times when it's not clear that we have to be on watch as our children's advocates to look closely for details that reveal the character of our daughter's friends. Hopefully your daughter has been taught by you to look out for certain things in her friends. Maybe between her, you, and your husband, the three of you can assess who your teenager can spend more time with.

First, not many guys will qualify for your high standards and be dating material for your daughter. Next, the opinion that "you try a bunch of different people on, and see who fits," is not a recommended exercise to my way of thinking. We all know that the more people you date, the more you're exposed to, and who wants that for their Christian daughter? Also, ever heard of baggage? And worse yet, scars? The leftover effects of "dating around" are usually baggage, at best, and you guessed it, scars, at worst.

I have found that the more fact-finding you do at the outset of the dating years or, more specifically, at the beginning of friendships, the less surprised you are later. There's always that boy who wasn't what he appeared to be, and unfortunately, he seems to have a lot of brothers out there. All this to say, hopefully your daughter will be drawn to and pursued by that boy who's a diamond in the rough.

Based on what we just discussed, you might be saying to yourself, "This crazy lady thinks you can find 'the one' when you're a teenager." I'm not saying you have to or that you're going to, but I will say that my family may blow the theory that you can't. Or, I should say, that it's uncommon to find your life's mate early has not been true in my life. Out of the five marriages represented in my immediate family, that's including our four children, and my husband and me, four of those relationships started in the teenage years. Four of the five couples were high-school sweethearts.

I do not think something's wrong if you don't find your marriage partner early. It may not be God's plan in your life to do so.

However, dating a whole lot of people, for a Christian, even an older Christian, is probably not the suggested route. Again, baggage.

So, back to the issue of a daughter's choice in dating. Let's hope now that she has totally been herself, meaning she has been true to her innermost character. This is extremely important, because with all the unknowns in dating, we don't need her possessing a habit of duplicity.

You see, one of the great things about falling in love is what we may learn about ourselves in the process. We find those tenets that we live by and things that are non-negotiable, like our faith in God and His Son, Jesus Christ. Other qualities that we've developed would hopefully be honesty, charity, purity, and integrity.

When one cares deeply about these behavioral traits, they are not drawn to someone who's flippant about something like personal integrity. If a boy has a problem with lying, that issue will come up, probably repeatedly, while dating.

The same thing is true of purity. If a girl is committed to being pure until marriage and the boy is not, that's a problem. Many times the boy will pressure the girl to cave in on her convictions about this. It would not be wise to date someone whose thoughts on this do not line up with hers. Her virginity is too high a price to pay to learn that he's not the one for her.

Save your daughter this disappointment and true heartache by not allowing her to even start dating someone so different from herself. Do your homework beforehand and know, as much as is possible, about the one/ones you let drive your daughter away from her safe and secure home.

8

I Think I'm Fallin' for Ya

Okay. Get ready. Let's say your daughter has started dating a nice guy, who you and your husband have cleared so far. Sometime in the first few weeks or months of the relationship, there will inevitably be a "what are you going to do?" moment.

This is commonly a challenge to the maturity of one or both people in the couple. It usually happens something like this: Another girl at school has really been flirting with your daughter's new someone. And we, being their mothers, are not surprised, because we remember high school. It hasn't been *that* long ago that we were in her shoes. Furthermore, we universally concede that frequently the most attractive person in the world is the person who's not available.

As soon as young people start dating, it's like the obsession of the school to see how quickly they can be broken up. It seems it's patterned after Hollywood. Who's dating whom? That's great!" Love it, love it, love it. Now, how can we break up these two? They're just too cute together.

Perhaps, there's that cute girl from Spanish class who has, all of a sudden, become aware that this "cutie patootie" is now taken. Let's call her Smoky. She saw him first, she thinks. He has flirted with her on more than one occasion, and she always thought there'd be time. Now, at this moment, she's got to make her move. "Surely, it's not too late," she worries. She gets in full-speed-ahead mode by smiling and batting her eyelashes in his direction. She starts hanging back, after the bell rings, so she can talk to him on the way out of class. Maybe his new girlfriend will see, and she'll be jealous. Maybe he will see that she's really the best one for him, not his girlfriend.

Now, Smoky may be "one of those." You know, the ones who are pretty, but who have ill motives. Dear Lord, help us. Boyfriend can choose one of several options. He can show he's not interested and quickly meet up in the hall with his girl to show Smoky she hasn't a chance. Or, he can flirt back with gusto. All his male hormones may be going "mach 2 with [their] hair on fire[3]." After all, he's got two girls after him. Maybe he wants to entertain the thought of being with Smoky, but he's really happy in his present relationship. If he doesn't want to discourage her, well, that's a problem. He's about to have a rude awakening with his girlfriend. This rude awakening is a line in the sand. It's gonna be a big deal.

Here's where many young girls make a huge mistake. First of all, there's nothing wrong with wanting to clarify, or as some people call it, DTR (define the relationship). What are we anyway? Are we exclusive?

The way she does this is critical. She has got to do this in the right way. The wrong way would be to say, "Why are you always talking and hanging around Smoky? You know she's a bad girl! I think she's been with half the football team. Don't you like me anymore? What did I do? Please tell me, I'll do anything to keep you. I don't want to lose you. I'll just die if I lose you." Can we say *rewind*? Don't be the girl who says these things. Don't ever be that girl.

Before going off the deep end, she could just make a mental note, think it through, and pray. She's noticed him paying attention to Smoky. Wonder what that's about? She should talk to him about it. Preferably not in the hall at school. So, later after school she says something like, "Hey, I noticed Smoky hanging around. What's going on with her?" Here's his opportunity to show he has no interest at all in Smoky. If he has no interest, that's great. If he acts defensive of Smoky or himself, proceed with caution.

That Foster Thing

This is where you want to show that you don't like her actions, and he might need to be warned that some girls are just Jezebels. Jezebel in the Bible was evil. We may be exaggerating here to define Smoky as evil, although to young girls, that's how they see the Smoky's of the world. Let's not forget, also, that girls know girls, if you know what I mean. Us girls can be fooled sometimes by guys but by girls? Never! Why is that? I think it's because we see ourselves in other girls. Sometimes, we see our worst self. In other words, we know we have the potential to act the same way.

Let's say he defends Smoky. Your next move is a defining moment. How you come across is critical as to how he sees you. A little competition is healthy, you might think. It may be. I do know a lot is toxic. The goal here is to let him know your thoughts, but don't start down a road of no return. That road leads to being single again. If you need to break up, do it. But don't let this lead you there if this is the only point of contention. Put differently, express yourself, but don't hang yourself in the process.

You want to show him that you're secure enough to not have a heart attack here, but that you feel a little possessive. I say a little possessive. That would be a capital L: Little. After all, we are going out, right? (This would only be appropriate if that has been established.) We called it going steady when I was a teenager. If you're not a little possessive, why do you call yourselves exclusive? And vice versa. If you're not exclusive, why are you acting possessive? You have no right to be possessive if you're not exclusive.

The Little, or mild jealousy part is just that you want to see if there's any interest in Smoky there. If he puts you at ease, your fears will be relieved. That means everything's fine. He can be a friend to other girls without being "besties" or egging on her flirting by his actions. You definitely don't want to be one of those girls whose boyfriend can't look up because you might think he's trying to look at another girl.

This is about mutual respect and a relationship that makes you both better people. If you've taken the first little bump and made it a nonevent, that's good.

It's the right time, now, to relay a little tool I read about in a book by Dr. James Dobson[4]. Dr. Dobson has written numerous books that I highly recommend. This tool represents people when they are in a relationship. Dobson calls it the Tender Trap, and he uses it for married couples and singles alike, in his book called *Love Must Be Tough*. For our discussion here, I think it is extremely helpful to couples before marriage[5]. The purpose of this tool is to show when someone is acting too needy. I thought it extremely valuable so I taught this concept to Kacey when she first began dating.

That Foster Thing

It goes like this: Hold up your two fists side by side in front of you. Keep your hands clenched, except your two forefingers, which you are now holding up side by side. These two fingers represent a girl; let's call her Demurely, and her boyfriend. Take one forefinger and move it one step (about an inch) out away from the other finger. This is her boyfriend (we'll call him Dreamy) doing something to move away from her. It can be anything from being overly critical or inattentive to all-out flirting with Smoky or anyone else. Now, take the other forefinger and move it one inch toward the other forefinger. This is Demurely. When she moves toward Dreamy, this is representative of her acting jilted and, therefore, going after what's rightfully hers. It can be her showing Smoky a thing or two. In other words, she tells Smoky to back off or else. It can also be anything that I will refer to here as being needy. Being a jerk to him or Smoky qualifies as acting needy. Also, throwing things. A fit, a cell phone … throwing anything in hopes of hearing a crash qualifies as acting immature and, therefore, needy.

All of these actions spell insecurity and, hence, neediness. Reacting so immaturely shows a fear of being left. Because being left would be unbearable to someone so devoid of confidence, that person *needs* to have this relationship at any cost.

Speaking of needy, I once worked with a girl who, upon hearing of her man talking to another woman, promptly cut the crotch out of all his pants. They were living together without being married, and suffice it to say, this was the beginning of the end for them.

Back to Demurely. She has an opportunity here to show maturity. If she does anything that appears to be pursuing him, it's a bad idea. She needs to evaluate the situation. What will she do? Put yourself in Demurely's shoes. Should you ask if he still wants to be together? Maybe you don't even need to go that far. Just clarify in a nonthreatening way.

You can express your insecurities in a way that's respectful. Something like this, "Hey if you want to date Smoky, let's just go our separate ways. No problem here. We can still be friends even. It seems like she keeps coming between us. I don't want to hold on to someone who really wants to be free."

If he says, "But I don't want to be with her; I want to be with you," then good. At that point, you bring forefinger playing Demurely back to square one. She now feels secure because Dreamy has assured her of his feelings for her. He has made his true wishes known, and she wants to stay with him, so Dreamy comes back beside Demurely.

This is actually a mature ending to the little bump in the road they just went through. If Demurely would've just taken a step back when she first noticed him acting interested in Smoky, she would've avoided some frayed nerves.

Taking a step away as pictured by the finger illustration would look like the following: from the square one position Dreamy would be one inch away from being beside Demurely. That's because he's done something to show his heart may be up for grabs again. Now, Demurely should move an inch in the other direction, not toward Dreamy. So now the illustration has 2 inches between the two fingers. This represents a lack of harmony in their relationship. In real life this would look like Demurely being too busy to talk to Dreamy after school, and also too busy to talk later in the evening.

Talking before going to bed at night is something that couples routinely do when dating. One last sweet nothing or "I love you" before going to sleep makes lovers have sweet dreams. For Demurely to miss this opportunity to hear from Dreamy one last time in the day should make him take pause.

Also, taking a step away could be her talking to some guy friend after school. She could later say that he was only a friend of her family's or her brother's pal. It would not be as threatening for Dreamy, but should make him wonder if she's starting to stray in her devotion to him. Something to make him a little worried after he's acted unattached is her goal. This should make him think twice. For couples who are mature and really want to be together, this is cleared up rather quickly.

After Dreamy has a little trouble sleeping that night he's super anxious to lay eyes on his girl at school and look into her eyes for signs of her feelings. When Demurely is quick to put his worries to rest they both feel a little closer to each other. They may even say a quiet thank-you prayer that they still have their sweetheart's love. In our finger analogy both fingers are back at square one, side by side. This is the preferred "keeping small things small" option.

Let's say, in another scenario, Demurely decides to "act out." Say she does something childish and possessive like crying and being overly dramatic, or calling him and hanging up when he answers. At this point, her actions say, "I feel so insecure that I'm retaliating." That spells needy. Anything that screams *mine* is too much. It looks like a two-year-old in a grown-up body.

This says a lot about her. She can be showing that she's desperate for him, and he might realize that he doesn't feel the same desperation for her. It can also be saying, "I'm not really ready for this relationship, because I feel like my toy is being taken away, and I want it back! Now!"

She is clearly not ready to be taken seriously in a mature dating relationship. All the while, Dreamy is seeing her in a different way. The independent confidence in her that he was attracted to at first is now gone. She's making a much bigger deal of this than needed. Who is she? "If she's this intense about a smallish thing, where will we go from here?" he wonders. Is she becoming someone who will want to control every aspect of his life? All he did was talk to Smoky, and now he's got a mad "wife" already.

Say he treats her differently now. He's totally turned off by her reactions to such a small thing. So he decides to act like there's more there with Smoky, and he pushes Demurely to get more jealous. Consequently, she has a choice to make. Does she just try to rationally get things back on track? She has been immature so far, so the chances of her being mature now are slim. Either way, he's taken another step away from Demurely. So, any childish action on her part = being needy. Being needy = following him.

The finger representing Dreamy is steadily moving inch by inch away from Demurely, and she is keeping up by moving toward him each time. What we have is her chasing him. It's a clear picture if you use your fingers, and guess what? It's unattractive.

It could, of course, be reversed where she's the one moving away and he's the one chasing her. Either way, it's pretty childish and damaging to the relationship.

These two either don't need to be together at all or they need a little coaching as to how dating dynamics work. If they are somewhat mature, they can learn that there's enough drama in high school as it is without bringing more. Dreamy needs to be honest about Smoky. He also needs to be honest about his feelings for Demurely. This can be worked out, and if so, they will come out stronger for it. It would be better, however, to just grow up and not bring all these theatrics to your school.

Now back to you. If these antics were experienced by you and your boyfriend, some objectivity could go a long way. The finger illustration allows you to look at what happened and evaluate without emotions. It would probably take some coaching and encouraging from a mentor to take the emotions out of it for a young girl. However, it's extremely valuable to be able to assess the actions of all the dramatic players. If you and your steady guy have problems that mirror what's described previously, then there's definitely neediness exhibited.

My recommendation is to not be needy. It would be almost impossible to filter through this kind of clutter to see how much the two of you are compatible in areas of faith, goals in family life, ministry, career, and free-time interests. Those are all important preferences to talk about. You are, after all, trying to find out how much you do or don't enjoy being with this other person. That's what dating is all about!

9

That Foster Thing

I also wanted to teach my daughter what I call, in my family, that "Foster thing." My maiden name is Foster, and my dad taught me to be proud of being a Foster. This included subscribing to the aforementioned Boy Scout traits, which were a given.

Naturally, my dad would want his own children to be good Boy Scouts. And two of them were, being boys and in our dad's Scout troop. Even though I was the only girl, I still knew what was expected of me. I knew that the trustworthy, loyalty, helpful, and so on list was somehow just the basics. And I knew that striving for excellence and virtue was a noble and honorable goal worth pursuing for a lifetime. I don't dare want to imply that my Foster family or I think we've arrived at that goal. It's always a work in progress with imperfect people, and the Fosters would be the first to agree with this.

Being a Foster meant being confident in what we felt was truth. Now, there are differing views on what is truth. As I grew and became a Christian, I realized that so much of what my parents had taught me was, in fact, straight from the Bible. And we know the Bible could be described as the Book of Truth. Actually it's the Book of Eternal Truth. Because of that, I knew those principles were timeless and were worth holding on to. Again, they were worth it for a lifetime.

Being a Foster also meant being comfortable in our own skin. This would not be in a haughty way. And definitely not in a snooty way. We believed in treating people the way we ourselves wished to be treated. It just meant being okay with who we were.

Who you are is a spiritually loaded concept. The Bible says in Psalms 139:13–14: "For You created my inmost being; You knit me together in my mother's womb. I praise You because I am fearfully and wonderfully made; Your works are wonderful, I know that full well." And that's *not* a Foster thing. That's a God thing!

The word *knit*, according to the dictionary, means "to make by interlocking loops of wool or other yarn with knitting needles or on a machine." Verse 15 of Psalms 139 uses the phrase, "When I was woven together …" One dictionary definition of *weave*, which is the root of the word *woven*, says, "to interlace (threads, for example) into cloth." Also, it says, "to contrive (something complex or elaborate) in this way."

Have you ever watched someone knit? That person does it one stitch at a time. It's intricate and detailed work that's interlaced together. The knitter does it with care and attention. They are making something specific and elaborate.

You were created by a Master Tailor as it were. Our Creator, God, put you together cell by cell. One commentary said, "Your physical being was knit according to a pattern of incredible purpose." Wow! Whenever you're feeling unloved, just take out your Bible and read this again. God cares so much for you because you are His design.

The Word of God says you were "wonderfully made." I know we don't need a definition of wonderful, but some dictionary synonyms are: "marvelous, magnificent, superb, glorious." Need I say more? I think you get the picture. You had a glorious beginning! If there was ever a reason to be okay with who you are, that's it!

In addition to the unfathomable truth that God has made us Himself, being born a Foster meant there was a family who loved me, probably even before I was born. (I certainly loved every one of my children when they each were in the womb.) I knew, even as a child, that I was wanted. My parents never treated us kids like the world revolved around us; however, nor was everything "all about me." We were just taught to have a healthy view of self.

We knew there were people prettier, handsomer, smarter, more athletic, and so on. That was okay. We were happy for them. They'd been gifted in this way or that. Guess what? You've been gifted too. My dad has always said, "You can have anything you want, if you're willing to work toward it and spend the time required to achieve it." I believe he's right. Sounds like another one of those timeless truths, doesn't it?

Being a Foster also meant being secure. This kind of security is enough to let people go when they want to be somewhere else instead of with you. It really is okay. Numerous Fosters in our family appear to have felt this same way. I don't know if it's in our DNA or what. I've just noticed it for years, and so I refer to it as that Foster thing. For most of them, it seems that trait has served them well.

That Foster thing has a few negatives. One would be that sometimes we might be too quick to think someone is not necessarily drawn to us and, therefore, not that interested in being our friend. If we think that, it would not be uncommon for a Foster to move on mentally. It's that "there are plenty of fish in the sea" attitude. It has also been described by an in-law as "you're okay to be alone." An in-law, by definition, does not have Foster DNA, so he or she might recognize this as a fault. Even though I am a Foster, I can see how that could be a negative. On the other hand, not being okay to be alone sounds kinda needy to me. By the way, I truly love all the Foster in-laws, every one of them! They make us better!

That Foster thing, for the main purposes of this book, would mean that you don't try to get people to be around you when they don't want to. You don't beg people to go with you somewhere, or visit you, and so on. This would also mean that you would get out of being exclusive with someone who doesn't feel the same for you that you do for them. We should want our daughters to want that too.

To explain, life is too short to stay with someone who wants to be away from you. Your goal in dating is to have fun, surely, but also, it's to discover if this person is that "one." The "one" is that person you really don't want to get away. That sounds a little needy, but it's not meant that way here. It just means that this could be it! That's assuming he's feeling the same way.

This is only *it* if both parties are drawn to the other the same way. That means you may find that "one" who makes you want to serve God more, and one day, serve him too. By this, I'm referring to the service that would be characterized in a loving wife for her husband. This blooming affection is something that's born out of a selfless relationship, and it keeps growing and growing. It starts slow, grows slow and steady, continues to be desired by both partners, and honors God all the while.

When the converse is true, and we've all seen these couples, one or both just go from drama to drama and from hurt feelings to more hurt feelings and ... baggage. It may even lead to scars that one or both

Baggage can be a lot to carry.

carry with them from that day on. It's sad to watch on the periphery and is similar to high school. Teach your daughter to be above the drama and to want a boyfriend who wants the same.

That Foster thing could just as easily, in your family, be that "Smith" thing or that "Jones" thing. The point is that you feel secure enough in whom you are to go it alone if that's the case. It means, not only in the arena of love but also in life in general, it's okay if someone decides to leave.

Now, I'm not advocating leaving once you're married. Marriage is a biblical covenant you enter into that says, "one man for one woman, till death do you part." That means you don't leave the marriage unless you're carried away in a coffin. This covenant is supposed to mirror God's covenant with the church where He says He'll never leave us nor forsake us. So a covenant marriage is more than a contract where both partners remain if certain conditions are met. A covenant is an unconditional commitment that promises to stay no matter the attitude, actions, or betrayal of the spouse. It's a sacred promise to each other before God.

Divorce is allowed in scripture for marital infidelity in Matthew 5:32 and 19:9. Even so, it doesn't mean divorce is mandatory after unfaithfulness, and in fact, reconciliation is always encouraged in Scripture. I've seen some marriages end well after going down the bumpy road that included betrayal by a spouse. To do so, however, requires a kind of forgiveness that can only be defined as godly.

Having said that, I realize there are cases where forgiveness could've been given, but the offender didn't want it and didn't care to work toward reconciliation. Let's face it, sometimes there's perpetual betrayal and ongoing abandonment. In those situations, divorce may be inevitable. At least there's a provision for the Christian in Scripture that can provide some consolation.

And so, we see way too many divorces in America today. Unfortunately, most probably were not precipitated by the thoughtful consideration discussed previously. I say that, certainly not to sit in judgment of those who have been through such a painful experience. I'm not implying they didn't consider their situation from a multitude of angles. I *am* saying two people involved in marital dispute probably aren't reading the Bible together to see what it says about reconciliation. It only takes one of the two deciding to leave for the union to dissolve, sadly.

As I mentioned earlier, those that leave their spouse are also leaving their covenant. So, I'm not talking about leaving a marriage here but a relationship or a blossoming relationship. You definitely should not stay in a relationship if you learn you're not right for each other.

Part of discovering who we are is made clearer by the loves in our lives. That is, not just our love for hamburgers over tacos

That Foster Thing

or patriotism over indifference but also our love for our future husbands over a guy we just dated a few times. Falling in love unveils so many discoveries but not just about the object of our love. We learn so much about ourselves in this process, and it's best not to deny what we're learning. In other words, take it as an email from God to your inbox when you unlock the true heart that reveals the real you. That would be your whole heart too. It's your very core. It's what makes you, you.

Do you see the enormity of this decision that you will eventually make that involves marriage? This is the rest of your life we're talking about. This is one man for one woman. Being who you really are and truly looking for the one person that God has set-aside just for you is a monumental undertaking. In other words, huge. You should never look at this lightly. God has a perfect plan for you. If it includes marriage, He has hand picked the right someone just for you. You don't want to miss His divine selection. Outside of your decision to trust Christ as your personal Savior, it's the most important decision you will ever make.

Now, if you fear you have married the wrong person, through prayer and the Holy Spirit's help, you need to try to stay in the marriage. I don't believe you bail out because you feel the two of you are incompatible. You have to pray the Lord will do heart surgery on you and give you a deep abiding love for your

Jerri Foster Schmidt

spouse. He can do it, and He will honor your commitment to Him and to your husband.

I believe it's a tragedy in heaven when a divorce occurs between Christians. We need to forgive, and forgive, and forgive again, as we already discussed in chapter three. God has forgiven us over and over.

10

To Forgive is Divine

I want to take a short detour now since we spoke of divorce at the end of the last chapter. I will not be writing a separate book to my granddaughters on marriage, so I want to tell them how important this subject is to me by addressing it here in this book on romantic relationships. It's not exactly about the mechanics of dating, to be sure. However, it's of value to dating people because it addresses the seriousness of a broken marriage. Marital union is, after all, the epitome of a romantic relationship. Broken marriages are much more devastating than breakups between daters. So, with that being said, read on about forgiveness.

Colossians 3:13 says, "Bear with each other and forgive whatever grievances you may have against one another. Forgive as the Lord forgave you." Most people want to be forgiven, do we not? Matthew 6:14-15 says, "For if you forgive men when they sin against you, your heavenly Father will also forgive you. But if you do not forgive men their sins, your Father will not forgive your sins." Wow! We don't talk much about the consequences of our unforgiveness, do we? To not be forgiven by God is the scariest thing we can imagine. Look at all God has forgiven us of. Is there any way to even count all the times we've messed up? No, there is not. We need to apply "What would Jesus do?" to ourselves, and then we need to honestly answer that question. He would forgive.

You can't help it if your husband chooses to leave you even after you commit to staying and loving. If he's the offender, don't be the one to leave if he truly wants to be forgiven. That's assuming he's admitted the transgression, sought your and God's forgiveness, and turned away from the sin. That's true repentance. Asking to be forgiven, but staying in the sin is not true repentance.

So, if genuine reconciliation is desired, then if possible, commit to staying. I recently heard of a woman who was asked how she avoided divorce throughout a marriage of twenty-five years. She promptly answered, "You just don't leave."

After all, the biggest tragedy if you leave is how you're treating your covenant with God. That's even worse than the pain you deal your spouse if he wants you to stay and has done his part to bring restoration.

That Foster Thing

My heart goes out to my divorced friends. Most did not do the leaving; their spouses left them. I know people in stormy marriages as I write this, and I just want to say one word: forgive. If possible, forgive.

Forgiveness. It's a simple concept, though not simple to do. It's practical, it's applicable, and it's profound. It's contagious and it's noble. It's small and huge concurrently. It's old-fashioned, it's newfound, and you are a class act when you do it. It's humility in action. It's the base, meaning it's something to build on, and it's the top. It's elementary, and it's collegiate. It can be done in nursery school, in board rooms, and on deathbeds. It's worth emulating, and it's worth teaching. It's liberating, and it's never frowned upon. It blows the mind and touches the heart at the same time. That means it flabbergasts you and pricks your soul in a tender way simultaneously. It can be done on battlefields and in foxholes. It's always done by lonely dogs for their negligent owners, by love-starved children for their absentee dads, and surprisingly, many times even by abused children. It can be done by maimed soldiers and paralyzed victims. I can pretty safely say it's always done by moms.

It can bring forth confession, repentance, restoration, a new hope, a new birth and renewed love. It can literally mend a broken home. It can be spoken but not practiced, practiced but not spoken, taken or left. Undone, it can dominate the mind and obsess the heart. It can be done immediately or after a lifetime. It can be pondered on a mountaintop and also while scuba diving.

You never reach a quota or do halvsies. It's either all the way or null and void from stagnation. It can calm the anxious heart, lower blood pressure, and probably cure cancer by providing such profound relief. It wets the eyes, sometimes with buckets of tears, because it converges love, peace, and relief together, often in an overwhelming crescendo. It truly covers not just a multitude of sins, but *all* sins, and we are obeying the King of Kings when we do it. We are never more like the Lord of Lords when we practice it. God was, after all, the Inventor of it. Because He did it for us, we can call ourselves His child.

It unleashes the power of God even when it's whispered, and the one who receives it never forgets it. It's usually followed by, "I forgive you too."

Do it for your children. Do it for your grandchildren. Do it for your great-grandchildren. Do it for yourself, do it for him, or do it for God. In the words of Nike, "Just Do It!" Just forgive. Please. Never underestimate the blessing that awaits if you do.

So, how does one go about forgiving? If you were to hear from people that survived a potential marriage-ender, would there

That Foster Thing

be some trick they could share? Would there be a way forward that allowed a grieving wife to put her heartbreak in the closet and magically forget it? Could she stash it under the bed with all the under-used exercise equipment and go about cheerfully? My guess is no. I've never experienced the pain from betrayal, so what I'm recommending was observed by me in others, not endured by me. It's been a blessing to witness those who not only lived through it, but had joy again with their spouse. God can "return the joy." I think *not leaving* is the way to implement this as I quoted someone a couple pages back. *Not leaving* and praying for God to work His magic could bring the healing one-day-at-a-time. Just maybe. Hopefully. By the way, forgiveness has not been an easy thing for me, in general, so what I'm suggesting here would be a giant spiritual undertaking for me. God was way ahead of me and had me marry the most forgiving person in the world. I've learned so much from him, though still not nearly as good at it. I believe a cry for God to forgive *through* one's own heart might be the only way. I believe He can do a supernatural delivery of grace right inside you. I don't know how He does this. How could any of us know how God accomplishes this seemingly impossible thing? It's God-sized. It's a stunt that man could never pull off. Man is too uh.... human. Yep, only God can do this. It's unexplainable, unfathomable, indescribable apart from Him.

I have literally seen homes put back together because of this principle of forgiving and staying. I heard recently that two-thirds of unhappy marriages reported being happy five years after doing this main thing of forgiving and just staying.[6] Wow! That's pretty powerful. I think it's just a huge confirmation of how God returns your love for each other when you honor first your commitment to Him. That's so like Him. It's truly a God thing!

11

Misery Loves ... Well, Nothing

Immaturity and selfishness are not pretty things to watch on any stage. We can observe them and ask why people act this way. I guess it should be no surprise that humans do what comes naturally. The natural thing is to argue and want our own way. Are these childish actions and reactions the result of being afraid someone is trying to change us? Is it because we're prideful or power hungry? Wanting the upper hand in a relationship is not recommended if one truly desires oneness.

I have seen couples who seemed to literally live on drama. They go from jealous rant to major argument to dramatic breakup. Then back to reconciliation and on to being mean to each other again. This cycle may repeat itself time and time again. Some went on to marriage and then divorce. Some went on to marriage and just misery.

Choose now to have a different dating story. Respect yourself and the other person enough to get out if and when you see you're not right for each other. If you don't notice that someone is not right for you, what does that say? Just do that Foster Thing. You'll be glad later. You may even thank me for introducing you to the concept.

Maybe you've had patterned to you nothing but fighting marriages; that's not what God wants for you. It doesn't have to be that way, and it shouldn't be that way. It is possible to be in a peaceful marriage where there's mutual love and admiration that flows back and forth between the spouses.

The tone for marriage is set in the dating years. So, respect yourself and the other person enough to work toward handling problems with maturity, not getting even. Don't be so desperate for love that you stay in a toxic relationship because you think it's better than being single.

People who think their marriage is going to look different than the courtship are fooling themselves. Most times, it's worse—sometimes a lot worse. People quit trying to impress after marriage because they've already caught the person. So, it could be that little integrity you saw in him between fights wasn't even real. Be very careful to honestly assess your relationship on an ongoing basis. A common mistake people make in bad relationships is thinking the person will change for the better after saying "I do." This almost never happens. Tell yourself the truth. Remember that it is better to be alone than stuck with the wrong person. In fact, I can't think of anything worse.

Another thing to consider in love and war:

The main reason to continue dating someone is that you're compatible. Some people may say, "Hey you're coming down pretty hard on those of us who have feisty and contentious romantic relationships! This happens to work for us." Well all I can say is, I'm glad you're happy, and if that works for you, then great. I'm not here to redesign working relationships.

An old movie comes to mind here. The couple has very different views of how to live their lives. He is a reckless rock star given to living large and on the edge. She wants to not trash her life. By the end, he has died in a crash brought on by an alcohol or drug-induced driving rampage in an expensive sports car. The final scenes are her singing a song about love.

You get the impression that this was real love. Not the way I define love, mind you. But you may say "Different strokes for different folks." Okay. I hear you. If sparring spouses "get" each other, then again, great. If they belong to some sort of Club of Contention where they have to have a strong mate who can go back at them when needed, then great. My point here is to focus on the compatibility of these two. If that's what you need and want, and he wants the same, then go with it. I don't believe, however, relationship drama like that is sought out or desired by most.

Most people want love that just works. You know when it does, and you know when it doesn't—work, that is. Prayer is undeniably your greatest tool for finding God's person for you. Love and life with that person will work. Don't ever forget that!

12

Mutual Respect

I said earlier that I would get back to the subject of respect. I think all God's creatures deserve respect. From little tiny babies in the womb to the elderly and everyone in between, people deserve respect. When you have that as a mindset, you will, hopefully, stop short of mistreating anyone. In dating, it can mean live and let live in a vein that says, "I won't try to change you." By the way, it's not your job to change anyone.

The Holy Spirit of God is quite capable of changing people. That goes for us too. If good and profitable change takes place in our lives, it's the Holy Spirit who's responsible for it, not us.

If you are submitting to the Holy Spirit's leading about your dating, you can also trust that God is the One who refines both you and your boyfriend's character traits. Your goal should be to "be conformed to the likeness of His Son" (Romans 8:29). A relationship born in heaven will be showcased by your mutual desire to be better for God and better for each other. If it proves true that one or the other of you do not share this goal, you should go your separate ways because you're unequally yoked.

Second Corinthians 6:14 says, "Do not be yoked together with unbelievers. For what do righteousness and wickedness have in common? Or what fellowship can light have with darkness?" This verse specifically says unbelievers.

We talked earlier about finding the right boy to date out of the masses. If you find your assumptions about his spirituality are wrong, do not, do not, *do not* continue to date him. You can fall in love with the wrong person just as easily as the right person. So, if you realize after dating that he is not completely sold out to God, get out of the relationship as soon as possible, and pray for your heart to heal from whatever feelings you have for him. Do not entertain the idea of him becoming the right person eventually so you can overlook this red flag right now. You will not be happy later for having convinced yourself of this!

The verse we just looked at spoke of being yoked together. A yoke is a wooden beam that is used between a pair of animals, sometimes oxen, so they can pull a load together. Their heads are locked in around the neck. Imagine if one of them decides to go another direction. The follower could go along, or he could resist and try to pull away. He could just buck up and fight. Get the picture? Any way you look at it, they have different minds on which way to go. So guess how successful they are at pulling this load? Not very. They're not accomplishing anything good at this moment.

Let's not overlook that being yoked with someone who is focused on going the opposite direction would be painful physically. It would be painful spiritually also. Leave it to God, in His Word, to give us such a visual picture of inevitable problems that come when couples have unequal goals. Conversely, if they are of the same mind, they can get their work done quicker because they're working together.

It's the same way in relationships. A couple can be better for God, in some ways, than they could be by themselves. For sure, in the area of marriage and raising Godly children, two parents working in unison toward living a righteous life is unsurpassed in childrearing.

Let's talk, for a minute, about the ox mentioned before that is just following. First of all, he's not pulling the same as the other, so the job suffers. He eventually either has to totally commit to the other's destination or else he begins to be a drag. He is physically dragging, and therefore, being drug along. This makes him a drag in several ways, if you get my drift. Anyone wanting to "go for God" shouldn't be dragging anything that will slow him down. So, to sum up this part, have enough respect for yourself to get out of the relationship with the person characterized by the willful ox.

When It's Over

Next, if you are the one in a relationship who is broken up with, or "ditched," as some people call it, respect yourself by handling it positively. It's better to keep it short and simple.

Do not demand to know what happened. Do not demand to know why his feelings changed. Do not ask what you could do that would make him stay. Do not ask if you could still hang out. Do not call him or ask all your friends about him. And <u>do not</u> take him back without a period of time going by and thorough conversation about your differences. And most important of all, <u>do not</u> take him back without God leading you to do so after much prayer.

A nineteen- to twenty-year-old girl once told me about her boyfriend breaking it off. She said, "He wouldn't tell me why he wanted out. I asked him repeatedly, and he never would tell me why." Now you can call this the Foster in me, but I thought she could've handled this another way. I was hoping she would see that it really didn't matter why. Continuing to ask why your boyfriend wants out makes you look desperate. Of course it matters to you why. But, and this is an important *but* in romantic relationships, if one-half of a partnership doesn't want it, the conversation is really just prattle. It's inconsequential. It doesn't matter. It's probably not going to change the outcome in the end. You could ask why once maybe. Maybe a better question would be "When did you know things had changed for you?" If he's not forthcoming with any detail that you want to clarify about something you said or did, then let him go. Gracefully. As if you could keep him anyway. You can't. Bottom line—you don't want to be with anyone who doesn't want to be with you. And demanding to know why a guy wants to break it off makes him see you in a needy way. You don't ever want to be viewed like that.

The Foster in me says to get him off your mind. Move on. Get distracted. Start a new project. Do things with other people. God will let you set your mind on something else. Ask the Lord to help you. After a while of purposely focusing away from your ex-boyfriend, the emotional pain will let up. The sun will shine again. Trust me.

Your reaction to a breakup can confirm to him that you weren't the one for him. Sometimes a girl can be too concerned with losing him to see that he wasn't God's person for her. And I totally see why she feels that way. It's because she has a broken heart.

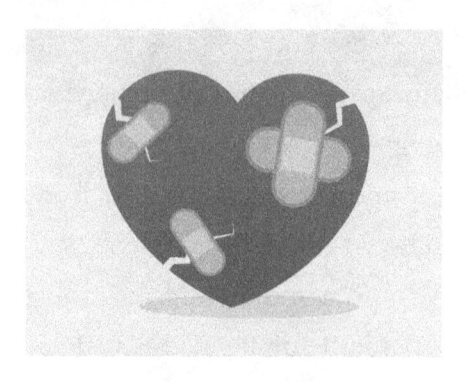

God is there for the brokenhearted.

That's when you can't be led by your feelings but by a common sense, self-respecting plan. God will help you get a vision of what that looks like for you. Pray, and ask Him. Jesus is truly your friend that "sticks closer than a brother" (Proverbs 18:24).

Finding your life's mate is the bigger picture. Dating is a means to that end. It's necessary, but it *is* the smaller picture. Try to focus on the big picture. Actually, you should be really relieved to find out someone's not the right one because of the timing of it. You're still dating, which means you're not married and finding this out. It means God has something or someone else for you who will be much better suited to you. Try to get a glimpse that His plan for you will be perfect for you. Let's look at Joseph again.

Remember how we talked about Joseph and his good choice to flee from sexual temptation? That was from Genesis 39. Well, fast forward, or just read the rest of Genesis, and you will see that Joseph goes from the pit to the prison to the palace. Chapter 41 verses 38–43 says, "So Pharaoh asked them, 'Can we find anyone like this man, one in whom is the spirit of God?' Then Pharaoh said to Joseph, 'Since God has made all this known to you, there is no one so discerning and wise as you. You shall be in charge of my palace, and all my people are to submit to your orders. Only with respect to the throne will I be greater than you.' So Pharaoh said to Joseph. 'I hereby put you in charge of the whole land of Egypt.' Then Pharaoh took his signet ring from his finger and put it on Joseph's finger. He dressed him in robes of fine linen and put a gold chain around his neck. He had him ride in a chariot as his second-in-command, and people shouted before him, 'Make way!' Thus he put him in charge of the whole land of Egypt."

So, we see how God's hand was on Joseph all the while. He suffered in the pit (Genesis 37:23–24) and in the prison (Genesis 39:20–21, 40:14–15, 23). Praise the Lord, however, because Joseph ended up as the Prince of Egypt. At the end of Genesis, we see Joseph's brothers apologizing to him for their mistreatment of him in throwing him into the well. Joseph shows Christ-like forgiveness when he tells them in 50:20, "You intended to harm me, but God intended it for good to accomplish what is now being done, the saving of many lives."

I'm sure that God makes no mistakes. He is your Advocate, as He was Joseph's. He will use everything you go through somewhere else down the road. If you let Him, He will enlighten or comfort someone else in need, someday. Through your testimony of His faithfulness, maybe you will be able to one day say, "You can trust Him. He has better things ahead. Don't give up." So hang on. Stay the course. Trust Him.

Back to love. I've also seen, repeatedly, these older girls, twenty-somethings and older, who, in my opinion, handle their love life from a perspective of neediness. Unfortunately, this sets them up for a breakup later on. To illustrate, let me go back about twelve years ago.

I was working, along with my husband, teaching young marrieds. I was talking with a thirty-something man who also worked in ministry in our church, but he worked in the singles area. I wondered if the single Christian girls were staying pure. He proceeded to tell me he was seeing time and again that they weren't. He said, "They're getting to mid- and upper twenties and are so scared they will miss out on the husband and the house with the picket fence." The house and the picket fence used to be thought of as the dream life. "So, what I see is them commonly giving in to social worldly pressure and relaxing their standards. That means either they're settling for dating a guy who is not right for them, and they know it, or they are compromising on their purity goals, or both."

That Foster Thing

Man can't build a dream life, only God can do that.

To summarize, if a young woman is caving to sexual pressure, her boyfriend's probably not right for her anyway. He's not leading her to be her best for God; thus, he's bad for her. This is certainly not his best for God either.

These poor girls are not only dating the wrong guy, but they're giving in sexually. That spells baggage. Most likely, these experiences will leave huge scars. I firmly believe that these individuals take away lasting negative consequences. At the least, it means intimacy given away and purity lost. At worst it can mean out-of-wedlock babies (which are over half of those born at the time of this writing) and/or sexually transmitted diseases. Sometimes it can drive a person to depression, self-esteem issues, inferiority complexes, and because of the aforementioned, even substance abuse. Let me elaborate further.

The first act of premarital sex can start a pattern and thus a lifestyle of promiscuity. That always leads to a debasing or "stealing away" of a girl's ability to grow in confidence. Remember how Adam and Eve hid in the garden after the first sin? Genesis 3:1–11 tells the story of sin's introduction on the world stage. After partaking of the forbidden fruit, Adam says in verse 10, "I was afraid because I was naked, so I hid."

For a girl to give herself sexually to a guy, she usually exposes her complete self. This means not just in a physical sense but also emotionally as well. To be discarded after laying herself bare and to feel the rejection after such intimacy would be devastating. The reality is that she gave everything she had to give, and that probably included her heart. To experience this, even once, would make one want to hide, just as Adam wanted to hide after realizing he was exposed. Let's not forget there was sin involved in his desire to be hidden. He felt vulnerable. And so does the girl who has been disrespected in this manner. Feeling vulnerable is the opposite of feeling confident.

Remember in the last paragraph I said the girl usually exposes her complete self when she engages in sexual intimacy? Well, I said *usually* because I think we also see sexually promiscuous girls become emotionally hardened and shut down in the area of true communion. They have to protect themselves from the inevitable emotional pain when yet another player does not treat them as anything special. So, they let themselves be used for the sexual act but don't ever reveal their heart. At this point they certainly don't feel love for this person who will be just like all the others.

This is a sad commentary on many young girls, women, and even older women's lives. Are they just looking for love in all the wrong places? Definitely. Especially in this age of sexual freedom and "anything goes with anybody," a lot of people "don't want to buy the cow when they can get the milk for free." The men in these scenarios don't think there's anything special about women who think so little of themselves. This practice that's so commonplace in America today is <u>not</u> sexual freedom; it's sexual <u>bondage</u>.

So, back to the problem of Christian females having to wait so long for their prince to come. They feel they've waited forever for the rider on the proverbial white horse to take them away into the sunset of romantic utopia. Maybe they worry that they'll be relegated to a life of singlehood. Oh no. First of all, it hasn't been forever. Secondly, if they fret about the idea of singlehood, either they're not called to it or they're not seeing how God is orchestrating their circumstances. Maybe. Plus, isn't God handling everything in His time? Let's get back to Realville. Remember, you have to be the right person to find the right person. There are no shortcuts to this principle.

My challenge to these young Christian women is *wait*. Pray. Pursue God and your God-given passions in career, vocation, and ministry. I do not believe a young woman would have the desire for a husband and family if God called her to singlehood. Why would God do that? So, if you have the desire, God is probably doing what He does best. That is, He's working all things out for your good (see Romans 8:28). And we know that His best is well worth waiting for! Our pastor, Dr. Adrian Rogers, used to say, "Happiness is something you find along the way in serving Jesus." Amen.

In the previous paragraph I said, why would God call a person to singlehood who has a desire for a husband? This is my opinion and is not written in theological stone. I said above that my personal recommendation would be to wait. Wait for God to bring the right person into your life. Waiting has value that goes way beyond paper to write its worth here.

My main objective is to reassure you that the Holy Spirit will confirm in your heart that someone is right for you or not. If you feel like you get the green light from the Lord, that doesn't mean you two will have a perfect marriage or a trouble-free existence. Waiting and praying can give clarity. The Lord can show you whether this is love or just lust. If it's true love, then by all means, order the wedding cake.

The reason I keep hammering at this is because we live in a sex-dominated culture. The animalistic passion characterized in modern media between unmarried people does not usually end in wedded bliss. It can. It's just not the norm. The preoccupancy with sex can certainly cloud a level-headed evaluation as to whether you and your boyfriend are compatible to each other for marriage. Most intimate couples probably don't have any trouble in that area. It's the taking and giving in all the other areas of a relationship that are undeniably harder. And so, the two may be thinking everything's great because they've been too wrapped up in each other in that way to notice anything else. Here we see another reason why intimacy before marriage is wrong.

If you and your boyfriend have made mistakes by going too far sexually, it doesn't mean that God can't change both of you and give you a wonderful marriage serving Him together. Many young people are not aware of God's purity standards before marriage, when they begin dating. Even many Christians don't know there's a better way to get to know someone than what's portrayed as expected in secular movies and television. So, waiting is good. Repeat that to yourself: waiting is good.

If, after waiting and praying, you feel the two of you should not pursue marriage, the time apart was a worthwhile thing. It stopped the intimacy, which can definitely lead to an undesirable result. Also, it gives space, which makes a breakup later a little easier to digest. Either way, you've given yourself some time to see if God wanted the two of you together or if that was just your idea.

Following a Dream?

I've also seen another disturbing trend in young women: when they quit jobs and move to other cities to be near guys they are dating without a ring on their fingers. I think it's fine if they're engaged. That scenario would be acceptable if he's building his career, the two get engaged, and they want to keep the momentum where he's got a future. That's provided they are not living together and will not do so to save money. While being money-conscious should be a main priority, God will not bless that if they violate His moral standards.

I believe that a guy views a girl so differently when she uproots her whole world and moves to be near him if the two are just dating. I think she's chasing him as described earlier. There is something inbred and natural in men that make them want to be the pursuer. For that reason, if the guy wants to relocate to pursue the girl, he's taking a chance, but okay. Her feelings might change because of it but maybe not. My main concern here is that she not do that. What if things don't work out? The jilted girl who has arranged her whole life around a guy who's left her is pitied. Pity is not attractive, and it usually evokes sympathy from onlookers. Please, for your own sake, let him pursue you enough to propose and put the ring on your finger before relocating.

I have to admit, as a mother of sons, I wouldn't be that keen on a son relocating because he was dating a girl. The circumstances would have to be just so to prove that it was the right thing to do, after much prayer, of course. I would only want that if he was about to get engaged and this was actually a confirming step in that direction. I still say I wouldn't want my daughter to do that.

There's another unspoken in the aforementioned breakup that looks bad for her. It's the inference that he couldn't go along with her planning their future, and he had to pull out. After all, she moved out of state to be near him. Outsiders might think, "Wow, she was *that* bad! He *had* to get away from her." Some men might go along with the plan, even though they're not gung ho, just to save her from embarrassment. They shouldn't, because that makes them staying with and possibly marrying someone they don't want.

Again, it reminds me of a scene from a movie. When asked why he got married, the guy said in a mousy way, "She said we had to break up or get married. So we got married."

That's right; let her be the aggressor. Let her be the one to say, "We've got to get married." No, no, no! Girls, hear me. Don't do that!

Sometimes these older (meaning marriage age) couples break up because the guy just "needs some space." Or he "needs some time." He just can't seem to catch up to her desires for marriage. So, they go on a break. Sometimes you will hear her say, "I think he's getting there. When he comes back, it'll be full speed ahead."

When I hear those words I hold my breath. I think to myself, I hope she's right, but I'm scared she's got it wrong. I'm wondering if he's looking for a way to get out without rocking her world.

I've seen girls so blind to it that they tell their friends, "I think we're getting closer, and things couldn't be better."

At the same time, he's saying to his buddies, "Man, I don't know what it is, but I don't think I can marry her." Then, after a number of weeks or maybe months, he pulls the plug and tells her good-bye.

This is why they call it going on a break.

She's devastated. She has put several years or sometimes more into waiting around for him to get ready.

Sometimes later you'll hear, "He's just not the marrying kind." You might even hear her say, "He has commitment issues. He just can't pull the trigger and marry the girl he loves. He's been through this before me, with another great girl, and he just couldn't bring himself to take the plunge."

Inevitably you hear later that this same guy met a girl, dated for a reasonable period of time, and *boom*, he did it. He proposed. He MARRIED HER. She's a great girl too. What did she do? I'll bet she let *him* do the chasing *and* the catching! Novel idea. It works. This is not about manipulating anybody. It's about being the best that you can be. It's about respecting yourself enough to be okay if this doesn't work out.

13

The X Factor

I believe this Mr. Nice Guy, from the end of the last chapter, doesn't know why it didn't work out. His ex-girlfriend has everything he's looking for in a wife. And she really does. Except one thing. She has painted a self-portrait by her actions that show something is missing. What is it? He probably still doesn't know. It's that X factor in dating. It's that "something" that has nothing to do with looks. It's that "way" about her that Billy Joel sings about[7].

"Don't know what it is, but he knows that he can't live without her." Do you know what it is? You might not know how to put your finger on it, but you know when it's there. Everyone knows when it's there. When it's not there, by definition, it's missing. It's precious. It's worth gold. It's a must. So, don't overlook it, (I'm not sure something that profound *can* be overlooked.) And don't lie to yourself and say it's there when it's not.

That Foster Thing

Those guys who couldn't pull the trigger and marry their steady are not so bad. I imagine they're just waiting for that relationship that has the X factor. Believe me, that one girl who's waited patiently for her Mr. Right is extremely grateful that he's available. As expected, he's glad he's available too. The fact that somewhere in his past he forged a painful breakup with someone who thought he was <u>the</u> one is old news. It doesn't worry the new fiancée. She probably thinks God saved them for each other. Maybe she's right.

The jilter's downfall came in being too weak to get out before she was dreaming of them at the altar. All because he was too nice? Hmmm … I'm not sure that delaying a painful breakup, and consequently causing *more* pain is being nice. Though he may not realize it at the time, he's making things much harder for her. Possibly he's just putting off something that he will ultimately conclude is unavoidable.

Guys need to be told it's a whole lot harder to break up after years of her thinking she's the one. It's much easier to do it when you first feel confirmed by God that it's not working for you. And girls, you should've noticed that something wasn't right before then too! You're being too needy if you're not really seeing the situation any better than that. Okay, okay, you might say, "Remember? Mindreading is not my strong suit." I hear you. I'm just saying a whole lot of people settle, and a whole lot of people are kidding themselves. Don't be in either group.

Girls, you want that "way" Billy sings about in your guy just as much as a guy wants it in his girl. Obviously. This is a two-way street. It's just so right and beautiful when both partners feel that way about each other. That's when you know it was made in heaven.

He knows that he can't live without her.

You feel you were made for him and he for you. All's right in the world when you discover this treasure—this treasure you've only heard about before. Maybe you've read about it. You've certainly prayed for it.

No honest person, knowingly or willingly, stays in a relationship that's not right for *both* parties. Again, I'm referring to the time

That Foster Thing

before marriage. After marriage, you're there. At that time, it's your job to love and serve your mate. So, get it right before then!

My prayer is that anyone reading this, certainly my precious granddaughters, will not settle for mediocre love. I pray they will soar with love that is best described as "meant to be." Ordained by God, hopefully their husbands will not only be the recipients of their affection but also just as enrapt. Most fascinated by their wives, then, like Billy Joel, they can say, "She's got a way about her, I don't know what it is, but I know that I can't live without her.

She has a way of pleasing. mmm... Don't know why it is, but there doesn't have to be a reason, anyway ...[8]"

Endnotes

[1] Woods, Ilene and Douglas, Mike. "So This Is Love." By Mack David, Jerry Livingston, and Al Hoffman *Cinderella*. Walt Disney Records, 1950.

[2] DeShannon, Jackie. "What the World Needs Now." By Hal David *This Is Jackie Deshannon*. Imperial, 1965. LP.

[3] From the movie *Top Gun*. Directed by Tony Scott. Paramount Pictures, 1986.

[4] Dr. James Dobson, Love Must Be Tough, (Word Publishing 1996) p. 30-33.

[5] Ibid., p. 207-209.

[6] Timothy Keller, The Meaning of Marriage, (Dutton, a member of Penguin Group USA Nov, 2011) p. 25-26 citing Does Divorce Make People Happy? Findings from a Study of Unhappy Marriages (American Values Institute, 2002)

[7] Joel, Billy. "She's Got A Way." *Cold Springs Harbor*. Family Productions, 1971. LP

[8] Ibid.